ETIQUETTE RULES!™

ETIQUETTE
AMONG FRIENDS

LAURA LORIA

rosen publishing's
rosen central®

NEW YORK

Published in 2017 by The Rosen Publishing Group, Inc.
29 East 21st Street, New York, NY 10010

First Edition

Library of Congress Cataloging-in-Publication Data

Names: Loria, Laura, author.
Title: Etiquette among friends / Laura Loria.
Description: First Edition. | New York : Rosen Publishing, 2017. | Series:
  Etiquette rules! | Includes bibliographical references and index.
Identifiers: LCCN 2016017412| ISBN 9781499464900 (library bound) | ISBN
  9781499464887 (pbk.) | ISBN 9781499464894 (6-pack)
Subjects: LCSH: Etiquette for children and teenagers—Juvenile literature. |
  Friendship in adolescence—Juvenile literature. | Friendship—Juvenile
  literature.
Classification: LCC BJ1857.C5 L67 2016 | DDC 395.1/22—dc23
LC record available at https://lccn.loc.gov/2016017412

Manufactured in China

CONTENTS

INTRODUCTION

When you saw the word "etiquette" in the title of this book, did you roll your eyes? Did an image of your grandmother pop into your head, telling you to chew with your mouth closed and keep your elbows off the table? While table manners are important, this is not that kind of book. You will not be learning which fork to use or how to curtsy. Etiquette simply means behaving in a way that makes other people feel comfortable. It is a part of the social contract: the unwritten rules that make society function as a whole.

Etiquette isn't always as simple as following the golden rule, or doing unto others as you would have them do unto you. It's really about being able to put yourself in another person's shoes. The question isn't, "Would I be OK with this?" so much as, "Would they be OK with this?" Attempting to understand another person's perspective is the key to good etiquette.

There have been rules for how to behave among others for all of human history. The ancient Chinese had rules about taking your shoes off before entering another person's home, which many people still follow today. In Europe, using forks was considered uncouth until the 1600s. Picking up food with your fingers was completely acceptable. Obviously, that rule has changed over time.

In the twentieth century, there were a number of etiquette experts who gave advice through books and newspaper and magazine columns. Emily Post was one such expert. Her 1922 book, *Etiquette in Society, in Business, in Politics, and at Home,* was a guide for living politely that emphasized kindness and courtesy. Her advice has been updated and modernized over the years, and her name is still

The key to a lasting friendship is understanding one another, through clear communication. This means both speaking with and, most important, listening to your friends.

associated with good manners today.

Others have followed in her footsteps. Judith Martin, known as Miss Manners, has written numerous books and columns about etiquette and was awarded the National Humanities Medal in 2005 for her work. Her style is formal and dryly humorous, and her message is no-nonsense. She frequently begs her readers to spend less time worrying about other people's manners and spend more time sharpening their own. Amy Vanderbilt and Letitia Baldrige are two other American authors famous for their writings about manners.

Advice columnists, while not specifically etiquette experts, have also helped shape our society's manners. Ann Landers and Abigail Van Buren, twin sisters, each provided expertise in social matters in their own syndicated newspaper columns for much of the second half of the twentieth century. Today's advice columnists include Carolyn Hax of the *Washington Post*, Amy Dickinson of the *Chicago Tribune*, and Pauline Phillips, who took over her mother Abigail Van Buren's "Dear Abby" column after her death. They counsel letter writers on the best ways to resolve conflicts with friends, family, and coworkers.

Good etiquette not only solves problems—it prevents them from happening in the first place. When you treat others with courtesy, you make them feel comfortable, safe, and important, and they are much more likely to treat you that way as well. Making, and keeping, friends is much easier when you are courteous and kind. It costs nothing, but pays great rewards.

CHAPTER ONE

WHO ARE (AND AREN'T) YOUR FRIENDS?

When you're a young child, everyone you meet is your friend. Everyone in your class at school, the kids on your tee-ball team, and children in the neighborhood fall into the "friend" category. Now that you're older, you're more selective about the people you choose to spend your time with. We treat people differently, according to our relationship with them.

Still, people your age you spend your day with are your peers, and they deserve your respect and courtesy, regardless of how close you are with them. We can divide them into several categories.

CLASSMATES

Classmates are the people you see at school every day. They may not be the people you like, or would choose to spend time with. However, you are thrown together with them for six or seven hours each day, whether you like it or not. So how should you treat them?

Everyone, regardless of how much you like them, deserves basic courtesy. This does not mean you have to be their best

7

Group projects can be tricky if you are paired up with difficult people. Being courteous and respectful will ensure that the work gets done to everyone's satisfaction.

friend, but it does mean your have to behave in a friendly way. What does that look like?

First, greet people by name. It makes them feel recognized as an individual and more likely to do the same for you. Second, be helpful when you can. It takes a few seconds to hold a door for someone, or lend him a pen, but it can make a huge difference in someone's day. Finally, give a compliment when it's due. If someone has a new haircut, tell him it looks good. If she gave a great presentation, tell her that you were impressed. You can always find something nice to say about a person, even if it's a small thing.

Courtesy for others doesn't mean you have to be close with everyone. There are people who might mistake your good manners for an invitation to close friendship. If a classmate is trying to get closer to you, there are polite ways to deflect her. If she wants to sit with you at lunch, you can say, "I'm sorry, I promised someone else I would sit with her." If he wants to hang out after school, you can tell him that you have chores to do. Politely refusing to advance the relationship further, while still being kind, is the best way to keep people at a friendly distance.

WHY SHOULD I BOTHER?

You might be thinking, "What's the point? I don't really like this person, or have anything in common with him. Do I have to go out of my way for someone I don't really care about?" The answer is yes, and here's why. Small courtesies make the world go round. These little interactions create a positive vibe, which puts people in a good mood, which makes life go more smoothly. Plus, it is always better to make a friend than risk making an enemy. Who knows when you might need a person's help at another time? Let's say you need help carrying a huge project to class. Who will be more likely to help you—the kid you ignored or the one you smiled and said hello to?

SQUADS AND BROS

Your parents might call this a clique or refer to them as "the gang." These people are your group, the people others identify you with. Maybe you all play on the same team, live in the same neighborhood, or share a common interest in gaming. They are your basic friend group, the people you spend most of your time with in and out of school.

Groups can be tricky. Sometimes they split off, or two people become especially close and exclude others. Other times, they become closed off, refusing to associate with people outside of the group. While having a group of people you can rely on is a good thing, it can quickly become negative if it isolates you from others or makes you do things that make you uncomfortable.

So, how can you maintain friendships in a group in a healthy way? Be open to other people as well. You don't have to do everything with your group. Maybe you have a group of friends in band class and another group to sit with at lunch. This is completely OK. If your group doesn't want you to hang out with anyone else, it's time to distance yourself from them. That is easier said than done, but if you limit yourself to one group, you eliminate the possibility of other friendships. People who have a variety of friendships are happier in the long run.

BEST FRIENDS

This is the person who you call first with news, who understands you like nobody else does. You share your secrets with him, and you know he won't tell. A best friend is a special relationship, but it only works if both of you are putting in the same amount of effort.

Friendships go through ups and downs, and best friendships are no exception. There will be times when a friend needs more from you, like when her parents get divorced or she doesn't get a part in the school play. You may have to put in extra effort, listening patiently as she vents her frustration and offering helpful advice. There will be times when you will need her support as well, so consider the energy you spend on supporting a friend as an investment in your friendship.

The basis of friendship is loyalty. Being supportive is a way to show a friend that you are on her side. When your best

Your best friend is someone you can rely on completely, and who can expect the same support from you. Mutual respect leads to years of friendship.

You don't have to face a bully alone. Rely on your network of friends, and your parents and teachers, to help you cope.

friend has a problem, of course you want to help him. It can have limits, though. If being loyal means putting yourself in danger, you have to protect yourself first. Let's say a friend wants to copy your homework. You might want to help him, but doing so could mean that you will fail if you get caught. In this case, saying no isn't being a bad friend—it's being smart.

ENEMIES

Wait—this book is supposed to be about friends! Well, friendships can go sour. As you grow older, you change, and so do your friendships. The person you used to swing with on the playground might become the person who makes fun of your clothes. You could have a falling out with a friend, who then spreads gossip about you, or tries to turn your other friends against you. How do you deal with this?

There isn't one good way to deal with unkindness. Sometimes you can ignore it, and it doesn't happen again. Other times, you can confront the person, and try and work it out. When talking about a problem with a friend, it is best to keep it one-on-one, or maybe have one mutual friend to help you work it out. It is also better to do it privately. People tend to show off or refuse to admit they are wrong in front of a group, so you might have better luck talking to them when they aren't at risk of being embarrassed.

When rudeness crosses over into bullying, however, it is time to seek help from adults. How do you know it's bullying and not just being mean? Bullying behavior has three characteristics. First, it is intentionally hurtful. The person bullying is trying to upset or harm you. Second, the person is in some way more powerful than you. This could mean that he is physically larger than you, or she is more popular than you are. Finally, it happens more than once. If a guy calls you a name one time in the hall, he is rude, but not necessarily a bully. If he does it every day and the names get worse and worse, this is bullying behavior. Tell your parents, a trusted teacher, the school counselor, or any adult that you think will help you, every single time it happens. Bullying is not always easy to see, so the more specific information you can give, the easier it will be to resolve the situation.

TEN QUESTIONS TO ASK A SCHOOL COUNSELOR ABOUT BULLYING

1. What are the school rules about bullying?

2. What is the line between teasing and bullying?

3. How do I report bullying behavior?

4. Who can help me when I am stuck in a bullying situation?

5. What are some strategies for dealing with a bully?

6. Can the school help me if bullying takes place outside of school?

7. How do I stand up for a friend who is being bullied?

8. What do I do when people make fun of me for "telling on" someone for bullying?

9. Is it ever a good idea to ignore bullying, or should I always confront it?

10. Are there antibullying groups at school that I can join?

CHAPTER TWO

I NEED A FRIEND!

Maybe you have recently moved and don't know anyone in your new town. Perhaps you have grown apart from your friends and are looking for new company. Making new friends can be intimidating, but it is easier than you might think. There are a variety of ways to begin a new friendship.

WHERE TO START

Cast a wide net when it comes to friendships. Joining clubs, trying out for teams, and doing community service are all good ways to meet people who share interests with you. However, don't rule out a potential friend because she doesn't like all of the same things that you like. Sometimes a new friend can open you up to new experiences that you might have missed out on otherwise.

Some people aren't "joiners"—they just don't do well in groups. You might think you are destined to be a loner and might think you're weird. You're not! Some people are just better one-on-one than in a big group. However, that can

Friends don't have to be clones of one another. Get to know people who might be a little different from you, and your life will be better for it.

make it a little harder to find a friend. You can find people you have something in common with by observing them. If you're into art, look around for someone who has interesting drawings on their notebooks. If you love manga, hang out in the library near that section. You're bound to find someone like yourself who might also have a hard time meeting new people.

WHY SHOULD I CHANGE? PEOPLE SHOULD LIKE ME FOR WHO I AM.

You should never change your beliefs or values to fit in with a group. It is dishonest, and you may end up with a group of friends you don't really like. You can, however, put your best foot forward when getting to know new people. In the first stages of getting to know someone, be positive and interested in others. If you disagree, do so calmly while acknowledging the other person's perspective. Don't dominate the conversation; give others a chance to speak. Be careful with jokes and sarcasm, because the person you're talking to may misinterpret what you're saying. Be yourself, yes, but be your best self.

HOW TO ACT

Confidence is incredibly important when you meet new people, but here's the trick: you don't have to actually feel confident in order to appear confident. "Fake it 'til you make it" is an old expression that applies here. People like people who seem happy with themselves and are drawn to them. Also, when you act sure of yourself, and people respond positively, you actually become more sure of yourself.

When you are looking for new friends, find a way to talk to them. It may be as simple as asking someone where the library is, or what the homework was. Learn how to tell when someone is losing interest in a conversation. If she

School is a great place to meet people, because it's easy to start a conversation. You already have something to talk about!

starts to look around the room, gives one-word answers, or doesn't ask you questions occasionally, she is trying to end the interaction. Try someone else, or try that person again another time. If he smiles, introduces himself, or keeps the conversation going, those are signs that he is interested in getting to know you better.

First conversations should be casual. No one likes a person who gets too chatty too quickly. It seems weird to people when you tell them your life story in the first five minutes of your meeting. Keep it brief, upbeat, and light. A polite person might listen to you blab on about yourself and then avoid you every time she sees you in the future.

A great way to make conversation with people you don't know is to ask them questions about themselves. People love talking about themselves; after all, they are experts on the subject. Ask them about their clothes, what they're reading, who their favorite musicians are, or anything else you can think of. Right now you might be thinking, "Wait. In the last paragraph, I wasn't supposed to talk about myself too much. Why do I have to listen to another person do it?" The difference here is that you are looking for a new friend, not the other way around. Showing interest in another person is a way to let them know that you are caring and unselfish—two important qualities in a potential friend.

KEEPING FRIENDSHIPS ALIVE

Once you begin a new friendship, how do you keep it going? You can't just ask them about themselves forever. Friendships are built on shared experiences, which means doing things together. Riding bikes, playing games, or shopping together are

Being active together, like on a challenging hike, is a great way to bond with friends and create lasting memories together.

ways to get to know a person better. Going to each other's houses and meeting your families helps as well. When friends do things together, they bond with one another and make shared memories.

One person can't keep a friendship alive. Friendship requires that both people make some effort. If you are the only person calling and making plans with someone, she probably doesn't value your friendship much. If you talk for hours about your problems, but don't want to hear your friend's complaints, then you aren't holding up your end of the deal. It won't always be exactly equal, but in general, both friends should be active in keeping a friendship alive.

CHAPTER THREE

ONLINE RELATIONSHIPS

So many of our interactions today are not face-to-face. Communications via e-mail, text, social media, and other platforms are the norm for many teenagers. While teens are often much more tech savvy than adults, they sometimes make social errors that they don't realize they are making. There is etiquette for online communication, for both politeness and personal safety.

It is a common stereotype that teenagers are always on their phones. A lot of that time is spent texting or messaging through other platforms, like Facebook or Instagram. According to the Pew Research Center, the average teenager sent and received an average of thirty texts per day in 2014–15, and 68 percent of middle-school aged teens used social media sites. As technology becomes a bigger part of our lives, those numbers will likely increase. This is why it's so important to learn how to use it properly.

SENDING THE RIGHT MESSAGE

When texting, there are a few basic rules of etiquette that everyone should follow. First of all, is what you're saying appropriate for a text? For example, texting a friend that you'll

THE GOLDEN RULE OF ONLINE COMMUNICATION

The most basic rule regarding communication online is this: if you wouldn't say it in real life, don't type it out. Because you aren't face-to-face, you might not censor yourself as much as you would if the person you're writing to was standing in front of you. It is a whole lot easier to be rude or to express mean things to someone when you can't see his or her reaction. Avoid the temptation to lash out at people, and choose your words wisely. Remember that everything you say online is permanent: once it's out there, you can never take it back.

meet her at five o'clock is a great use of text messaging. You're communicating a small piece of information efficiently. However, there are some conversations that are not meant for texting. Long back-and-forth conversations about serious matters are best kept to phone calls or in-person conversations.

Next, watch what you type! Spelling and grammar count in texts, too. Abbreviations or shortened spellings are OK when you're texting friends, but be sure to use punctuation and proper grammar when possible. It makes your message clear and prevents misunderstandings.

While you're reading over your message before you hit send, there are a few things to look for. Always double check to whom you are sending it! This can prevent an embarrassing situation, like spoiling a surprise or accidentally sharing a secret. Also, check to see if your tone is clear. You might think you're being funny, but the person reading it might not get that. Emojis can help convey the kind of "voice" you're using.

Finally, when is it OK to text? Consider your surroundings. The people around you are more important than the message on your phone. If you are with friends, don't spend all of your time texting other friends. It's rude, because it makes the people you're with feel like they're not important to you. Where are you? Texting while you're watching a movie at home is fine, but it definitely isn't in the movie theater. You may think you're being discreet, but the whole theater can see your screen light up, and it is extremely distracting. Other places where texting is not OK are at a church, performance,

Texting is quick and convenient, but it's not always the best way to communicate. Some things are best said face-to-face.

the dinner table, or during class. It's hard for everyone, not just teens, to resist the temptation to check their messages when their phone buzzes. In no-text zones, shut it down and put it away. The texts will be there when you're done!

PRESENTING YOURSELF ONLINE

Social media communications are a little different than texting. Usually, you are making a statement for your friends or followers to see. You are often sharing images as well on social media. Keep you posts clear, positive, and appropriate. You never know who will see them. Even if you think your privacy settings are enough, the truth is you can't prevent people from taking screenshots and sharing them with anyone they wish. Also, when you post pictures, it's a good idea to ask any other people in the picture for permission first. Some people might not be comfortable with it, and you should respect their wishes.

Cryptic posts, like "Ugh! Worst day ever!," can be seen as attention-seeking or overly dramatic. Without more information, people might perceive you as whiny or obnoxious. It's acceptable to express your feelings in a post, but if your page is full of statements like this, you might find people start to avoid you online. Social media sites are also not the place to have arguments with others. Disagreements are best handled in person and can spiral out of control online when other people begin to comment.

GAMING SAFELY

Another place teens communicate online is through gaming, whether on a phone, computer, or gaming console. Often, you are playing with people you don't know in real life. In these cases, watching what you say is doubly important. Never tell strangers online your full name, age, or where you live, for your own safety. You may think you are playing with a peer when it is actually an adult. It is also important to watch your language. Not only is it rude to curse excessively, but it can also get you blocked or removed from some games. Competitive situations can get heated, so keep yourself in check to ensure that you can keep playing.

Competition gets people fired up, so don't forget your good sense. Never share personal information online, keep it clean, and sign off if it gets out of control.

Even if you are unfailingly polite online, other people might not be. What can you do? The nice thing about online communication is that you can easily disconnect. If you don't like what someone says, you can hide him, block him, or log off. However, if things escalate or they harass you, take it seriously. Take screenshots or save conversations, and show a trusted adult. Cyberbullying is a real problem and should be handled by the trusted adults in your life, just like in-person bullying would be.

MYTHS AND FACTS ABOUT TEXTING

MYTH: It doesn't really matter what I say—they know what I mean.

FACT: Words matter, and texting is no exception. People won't know what you mean if you don't say it clearly. Confusing or mysterious texts can damage relationships.

MYTH: Group texts are the best way to let everyone know what's going on.

FACT: Group texts can be helpful sometimes, but they can get annoying quickly as everyone replies. Use them only when there's no other good way to get your message across. Texting the whole soccer team that the field location has changed is one example of a good group text.

MYTH: It's fine to be late to meet someone as long as I text them.

FACT: Everyone runs late sometimes, and it is polite to let people know about it. However, texting doesn't excuse the lateness. Being on time shows people that you respect them, so don't use texting as a substitute for being punctual.

CHAPTER FOUR

ON THE HOME FRONT

For most teens, having one or more friends visit your house is pretty common. You can and should relax at your house, but that doesn't mean you should forget your manners. Being a good host makes your friends comfortable and more likely to return. There are a few easy ways to do this.

HOSTING ETIQUETTE

When a friend comes over for the first time, help him get oriented. Introduce him to your parents and siblings. If you have pets, introduce them as well. Some people are uncomfortable with animals; if you notice that your friend seems wary of your dog or cat, put it in another room. Show him where to put his belongings, and point out where a few important things are located, like the phone or the bathroom. If there are off-limits rooms in your home, like other people's bedrooms or a home office, be sure to tell him that, too, so he doesn't wander in accidentally.

Alert your friend to any house rules that are important to know, like taking off shoes or not swearing. Your friend doesn't

Greet your friend at the door—don't just holler for her to come up to your room. It will put her at ease, especially if it's a first visit.

want to unintentionally upset your parents simply because he doesn't know how your house works. Every family is different, and your friends will understand that these aren't your rules, but you have to communicate them. Parents can be embarrassing, but everyone has them. Your friends get it.

UNFAMILIAR SURROUNDINGS

If you and your friends come from different cultural or religious backgrounds, give them some advice before they come over or you visit them. If one of your family members doesn't speak English, tell your friend, so she won't think that the person doesn't like her because he or she isn't making conversation. If your religion prohibits certain foods or requires a certain dress code, let your friend know so he can plan for it. If you are the visitor, ask questions before you go. Your friend is the best resource for information about her family and will do her best to prepare you. Above all, don't worry about making a mistake. People usually understand if you goof up and will help you do things the right way.

Customs or foods that are unusual to you are everyday life for other people. Let your host teach you something new. You'll feel more comfortable if you join in.

FAMILY MATTERS

Your parents will want to get to know your friends a bit when they come over. Teenagers can be shy around adults they don't know or give one-word answers. Help your friend out by telling your parents a little about her before she comes over. When you introduce them, help the conversation along by mentioning interesting things about her that your parents can comment on. If you sense your friend is getting uncomfortable, find a way to excuse yourselves to another room. Your friend will be looking to you for cues on what to do, so help her out.

If you have siblings, they will probably be interested in your visitor as well. Even if they are annoying, treat them with courtesy. After all, it's their house too. It's nice to include them in your activities if you can, even if just for a little while. While you might find your little brother obnoxious, your friend might think he's hilarious. If a sibling is really getting in your way, there are a couple of things you can do to avoid it in the future. One, ask your parents for help. Maybe one of them can do another activity with her while your friend is there. If that's not an option, strike a deal. Offer to do one of your brother's chores or let your sister borrow your favorite shirt if they'll agree to leave you alone. It's best to strike these deals before the visit, or you'll be stuck negotiating in front of your friend.

ENTERTAINING

You might just invite a friend to "hang out" at your house, but that doesn't mean you shouldn't have a plan. Decide beforehand on a few activities you might do together so you aren't

Even if you're just watching videos on YouTube, you can interact with your friend. Compose comments together, or take turns showing each other your favorite channels.

bored. Playing games, making art, listening to music, or cooking something together are all casual activities that can be fun to do and are social. Sitting on the couch and watching TV is acceptable too, but make sure that you do something interactive during your visit. Above all, be flexible. Your guest should get to make choices about what to do. Present a few options, but let him choose the activity. He'll likely do the same for you when you go to his house.

GUEST ETIQUETTE

When you are the guest, be the kind of guest that will get invited back. Introduce yourself to the family if your friend doesn't. Watch how she behaves and act similarly or even a little more politely. No one ever looks down on you for being too nice. Treat siblings kindly, even if your friend doesn't. His parents will be much more likely to invite you back if you do. If you're unsure about anything, just ask. It's much less embarrassing to ask where the bathroom is than to stumble into it when someone else is using it!

When you are the guest, be flexible. If you prefer fruit for a snack, but your friend offers you something different, you can either eat it or say "No thanks," but don't just help yourself to whatever is in the cupboards. Let your host be your guide. If you don't like an activity your host has planned, it might be a good idea to try it anyway. Either you'll find that you like it after all, or you'll be a good sport for trying.

EXIT STRATEGIES

If you're not having a good time, or you and your friend fight, how can you leave politely? It's a good idea, for your first visit to someone's house, to keep it short. You can say you have homework, or practice, or come up with another reasonable excuse. If it's a friend you know well, you can plan longer visits, and be a little more up front. It's perfectly fine to say that you're tired and need to go home. If a friend is staying with you for an extended period of time, like for a weekend, it's all right to take a break from each other for a while. Also, a change of scenery might help if you get sick of each other: go outside, walk to the library, or throw a ball around.

CHAPTER FIVE

ON THE TOWN

Hanging out with your friends can take place in many different settings. It's important to know how to act so that everyone can have a good time.

RESTAURANTS

When going out to eat with friends, be prepared. Choose a restaurant everyone likes. If it's a fast-food place, each person can order and pay individually. At a table service establishment, when you order, be polite to your server. If you're sharing a dish with a friend, ask for an extra

Sharing a meal with someone is a great experience if everyone knows how to act at a restaurant. Choose your dining partners carefully.

plate and divide the food fairly. Keep your table tidy, and if you need something, ask the other people at the table if they need anything before you get your server's attention, so you aren't sending her back and forth to the kitchen numerous times.

Paying the bill at the end of the meal can be awkward. Bring more money than you think you will need, just in case it's more expensive than you expected. If you only want to pay for what you got, ask if it is possible to get separate checks before you order. If you are splitting the check, make sure you put in the correct amount of money toward the bill. Don't forget to tip: at least 15 percent for good service or more for great service. Everyone should chip in for this. Tipping is customary at a restaurant.

SHOPPING

Visiting a mall with friends can be a great experience, but it can also be tricky. Decide beforehand if you are window-shopping, or if you have things you need to buy. Take turns with friends choosing which stores to go to. When you're in a store, leave things as you found them. Don't make a mess of the merchandise—this is why some storeowners don't like teen-age customers. It is likely that you could have a job in a mall at some point, so put yourself in the worker's place. Would you want to clean up after you?

When a friend asks your opinion about something she might buy, be honest but kind. If the shirt she's trying on looks terrible, show her something else that you think would look better. Don't make fun of or belittle her choices. People have different tastes, and just because you don't like it doesn't mean she shouldn't get it if she does. It's most important that he or she is comfortable and confident in the outfit.

Shopping with friends is a great way to get to know them better, and it may give you ideas for what to get them for a birthday present later.

One uncomfortable situation that might come up is if a friend steals something. If they ask you to help, refuse and leave the store immediately. If he is caught, you could be suspected of being his accomplice and get in just as much trouble. People steal for lots of reasons: for fun, because they can't afford something, or they think that it's not a big deal. No

GETTING THERE

One problem with going out with friends is getting there. Many teens live in places where walking is inconvenient, dangerous, or impossible because of distance. Arranging transportation is your responsibility when you make plans. Never go anywhere without knowing how you will get home. Maybe your parents can drive one way, and your friend's parents can bring you home. In some places, you can take public transportation or taxi to get where you're going. No matter how you get there, arrange your transportation both ways before you go out. You don't want to inconvenience your parents, or your friend's parents, with your lack of planning. They may not be available, or have enough room in the car for you, and then you're stuck!

matter the reason, it is always wrong. A friend who wants you to shoplift is one you should never go to a store with again.

ACTIVITIES

Other fun places to hang out include laser tag arenas, amusement parks, and bowling and trampoline centers. A recreational activity is usually a group activity, which requires some planning in advance.

Set a place and time to meet up with all of your friends. The main entrance is usually easiest for everyone. When

Pick an activity that everyone in your group can enjoy. For snowboard-ing, a more experienced rider could give a lesson to a newbie.

you're in, it is easy to get separated. Make sure everyone knows when and where you'll be meeting again. If people want to split up, you could say, "Let's meet at the snack stand in an hour." That way you can keep track of one another, and make sure everyone is safe and having a good time.

It's easy to get overexcited at high-energy places, but try to be considerate of other patrons. Walk in pairs, so you're not taking up the whole aisle. Never line jump; if your friends want to ride with you, join them at the end of the line. Keep your volume reasonable. Other people don't need to hear your conversations!

It's natural that, in a group activity, people will split off into pairs or trios. Make sure no one is left out, and try to spend some time with all of the people in your group.

PARTIES

Parties can be held at homes, restaurants, or event facilities. When you receive an invitation, be sure to RSVP, or reply whether or not you can attend, as soon as possible. It helps your host plan how much food to have and is the best way to ensure that you'll be invited again. If it's a casual party, ask if you can bring some chips or soda, or maybe a game or some music. Figure out what to wear before the day of the party. Shorts and leggings are usually fine for an at-home birthday, but they'll be too casual for a bar mitzvah or quinceañera. Ask your friend what he's wearing if you're not sure.

At the party, be a good guest. Aside from following house rules, it is your job to have fun. Your host will worry about you if you sit in a corner all night and she won't be able to tend to her other guests. Talk to lots of different people. Participate in games. If you're shy, or don't know anyone, volunteer to take pictures. It gives you an excuse to approach people. Offer to help clean up after. Even if your host says no, you'll be remembered as a polite guest and invited back for the next party.

Interacting with friends in different settings has unique challenges and expected behaviors. In any situation, if you are friendly, straightforward, and enthusiastic, you'll be fine.

GLOSSARY

accomplice One who helps another commit a crime.

anonymous To keep one's identity secret; remain unknown.

appropriate The proper or correct thing to do.

bullying To intimidate, threaten, or harm someone repeatedly.

censor To omit or limit one's words.

cliché A tried and true saying that is often overused.

cryptic Something that is intentionally unclear.

customary What is usually expected in a situation.

deflect To focus attention away from something or someone.

escalate To move up to the next level.

inconvenience To make something more difficult for someone.

merchandise Items for sale in a store.

negotiating Working things out or making an agreement
     between people.

oriented Knowing your surroundings; figuring out where you are.

patrons Paying customers at a place of business.

peer Another person of the same age or position as yourself.

perceive How someone sees something; point of view.

perspective A person's understanding of another's actions.

punctual On time; respectful of other's time.

receptive Open and accepting of other's ideas.

recreational Activities designed for fun and entertainment.

FOR MORE INFORMATION

Boys and Girls Clubs of America
1275 Peachtree Street, NE
Atlanta, GA 30309
(404) 487-5700
Website: http://www.bgca.org/whatwedo/HealthLifeSkills/Pages/
    HealthLifeSkills.aspx
Programs available at the Boys and Girls Clubs include Passport to
    Manhood, a character education group, and NetSmartz, which
    emphasizes age-appropriate internet usage.

Boys and Girls Club of London
184 Horton Street East
London, ON N6B 1K8
Canada
(519) 434-9114
Website: http://www.bgclondon.ca
This organization offers the Keystone Club, which teaches
    leadership and good decision-making skills.

Bullying Canada
471 Smythe Street
P.O. Box 27009
Fredericton, New Brunswick E3B 9M1
Canada
Website: https://www.bullyingcanada.ca
The Bullying Canada organization maintains a twenty-four-hour
    hotline teens can call for advice on dealing with bullying.

Girl Talk
3490 Piedmont Road, NE
Suite 1104
Atlanta, GA 30305
Website: http://www.mygirltalk.org
Girl Talk can help people set up peer mentoring groups in their

community, so high school girls can help middle school girls with their leadership and social skills.

National Bullying Prevention Center
PACER Center, Inc.
8161 Normandale Boulevard
Bloomington, MN 55437
(952) 838-9000
http://www.pacerkidsagainstbullying.org/kab
The National Bullying Prevention Center offers advice and materials to prevent bullying for kids.

Smart-Girl
155 Inverness Drive West
Suite 200
Englewood, Colorado 80112
(303) 999-2340
Website: http://www.smart-girl.org
One of Smart-Girl's goals is to build group social skills for girls aged ten to fourteen.

WEBSITES

Because of the changing number of internet links, Rosen Publishing has developed an online list of websites related to the subject of this book. This site is updated regularly. Please use this link to access this list:

http://www.rosenlinks.com/ER/friends

FOR FURTHER READING

Black, Rebecca. *Electronic Etiquette: Cell Phones, Netiquette, Social Media…Oh My.* North Charleston, SC: CreateSpace Independent Publishing Platform, 2015.

Black, Rebecca. *Etiquette for the Socially Savvy Teen: Life Skills for All Situations.* North Charleston, SC: CreateSpace Independent Publishing Platform, 2015.

Cannon, J.J. *@Sophie Takes a #Selfie—Rules & Etiquette For Taking Good Care Before You Share.* Longboat Key, FL: Telemachus Press, 2014.

Crist, James. *The Survival Guide for Making and Being Friends.* Golden Valley, MN: Free Spirit Publishing, 2014.

Criswell, Patti. *A Smart Girl's Guide: Friendship Troubles (Revised): Dealing with Fights, Being Left Out & the Whole Popularity Thing.* Middleton, WI: American Girl, 2013.

Donovan, Sandy. *Communication Smarts: How to Express yourself Best in Conversations, Texts, E-mails and More.* Minneapolis, MN: Twenty-First Century Books, 2012.

Dupree, Toni. *Whose Fork is it Anyway? Dining Etiquette for Teens.* Seattle, WA: Amazon Digital Services, 2015.

Fine, Debra. *Beyond Texting: The Fine Art of Face-to-Face Communication for Teenagers.* New York, NY: Canon Publishers, 2014.

Forest, Scott. *The Kid's Guide to Sports Ethics.* Mankato, MN: Capstone Press, 2014.

Holyoke, Nancy. *A Smart Girl's Guide: Drama, Rumors & Secrets: Staying True To Yourself in Changing Times.* Middleton, WI: American Girl, 2015.

Joiner, Whitney, and Haley Kilpatrick. *The Drama Years: Real Girls Talk About Surviving Middle School—Bullies, Brands, Body Image, and More.* New York, NY: Free Press, 2012.

Kimball, Marrae. *The Secret Combination to Middle School.* Norway, ME: Find Your Way Publishing, 2013.

Klein, Rebecca. *Frequently Asked Questions About Texting, Sexting, and Flaming.* New York, NY: Rosen Publishing Group, 2013.

Manecke, Kirt. *Smile & Succeed For Teens: A Crash Course in Face-to-Face Communication.* Milford, MI: Solid Press, 2014.

Mayrock, Aija. *The Survival Guide to Bullying: Written by a Teen.* New York, NY: Scholastic, 2015.

McIntyre, Thomas. *The Survival Guide for Kids with Behavior Challenges: How to Make Good Choices and Stay Out of Trouble.* Golden Valley, MN: Free Spirit Publishing, 2013.

O'Toole, Jennifer Cook. *The Asperkid's (Secret) Book of Social Rules: The Handbook of Not-So-Obvious Social Guidelines for Tweens and Teens with Asperger Syndrome.* Philadelphia, PA: Jessica Kingsley Publishers, 2012.

Skeen, Michelle. *Communication Skills for Teens: How to Listen, Express, and Connect for Success.* Oakland, CA: Instant Help, 2016.

Subramanian, Mathangi. *Bullying: The Ultimate Teen Guide.* Lanham, MD: Rowman & Littlefield, 2014.

Tayleur, Karen. *Manners!* North Mankato, MN: Stone Arch Books, 2014.

BIBLIOGRAPHY

Alford, Henry. *Would it Kill You to Stop Doing That?* New York, NY: Hachette Book Group, 2012.

Baldrige, Letitia. *Letitia Baldrige's New Manners for New Times.* New York, NY: Scribner, 2003.

Carnegie, Donna Dale. *How to Win Friends and Influence People for Teen Girls.* New York, NY: Fireside, 2005.

Cassada Lohmann, Raychelle. "Mean vs. Bullying." *Psychology Today*, November 23, 2012 (https://www.psychologytoday.com/blog/teen-angst/201211/mean-vs-bullying).

Coles, Joan M., and Elizabeth L. Post. *Emily Post's Teen Etiquette.* New York, NY: Harper Collins, 1995.

Cultural China. "Etiquette." Cultural China, 2014 (http://traditions.culturalchina.com/en/15T2786T8003.html).

Dougherty, Karla. *The Rules to Be Cool: Etiquette and Netiquette.* Berkely Heights, NJ: Enslow Publishers, 2001.

Lenhart, Amanda. "Mobile Access Shifts Social Media Use and Other Online Activities." Pew Research Center, April 9, 2015 (http://www.pewinternet.org/2015/04/09/mobile-access-shifts-social-media-use-and-other-online-activities/).

Martin, Judith. "About Judith Martin/Miss Manners." Miss Manners, 2016 (http://www.missmanners.com/home/about-miss-manners.html).

New York Times. "Emily Post is Dead Here at 86; Writer was Arbiter of Etiquette." September 27, 1960 (http://www.nytimes.com/learning/general/onthisday/bday/1003.html).

Packer, Alex J. *How Rude!* Minneapolis, MN: Free Spirit Publishing, 2014.

Packer, Alex J. *The How Rude Handbook of Family Manners for Teens.* Minneapolis, MN: Free Spirit Publishing, Inc., 2004.

Post, Emily. *Teen Manners: From Malls to Meals to Messaging and Beyond.* New York, NY: Collins, 2007.

Rhodes, Jesse. "Renaissance Table Etiquette and the Origins of Manners." Smithsonian Institute, March 29, 2011 (http://www.smithsonianmag.com/arts-culture/renaissance-table-etiquette-and-the-origins-of-manners-31348606/?no-ist).

INDEX

ABOUT THE AUTHOR

Laura Loria is a writer and teaching assistant in a junior-senior high school in upstate New York. She holds a bachelor's degree in elementary education and has worked with children of all ages for more than twenty years. She is also the mother of two tweenage children, a thirteen-year-old boy and a ten-year-old girl.

PHOTO CREDITS

Cover, pp. 7, 15, 22, 28, 34 (top) antoniodiaz/Shutterstock.com; cover (bottom) Martin Dimitrov/E+/Getty Images; p. 5 PhotoObjects.net/Thinkstock; p. 8 Ingram Publishing/Thinkstock; p. 11 LiudmylaSupynska/iStock/Thinkstock; p. 12 © iStockphoto.com/hjalmeida; p. 16 vadimguzhva/iStock/Thinkstock; p. 18, 32 moodboard/Thinkstock; p. 20 Don-Land/Shutterstock.com; p. 24 © iStockphoto.com/Karin Lau; p. 26 iStockphoto.com/dgmata; p. 29 Jean-philippe Wallet/iStock/Thinkstock; p. 30 DragonImages/iStock/Thinkstock; p. 34 (bottom) Brand X Pictures/Stockbyte/Thinkstock; p. 36 william87/iStock/Thinkstock; p. 38 Karl Weatherly/DigitalVision/Thinkstock.

Designer: Michael Moy; Editor: Heather Moore Niver; Photo Researcher: Heather Moore Niver